1

Table of Contents

INTRODUCTION

Electricity is a very important component of the construction of a house. Lights, appliances, air conditioning and heating, and security systems all run on electricity. Electrical wiring is essential to installing electricity in a house. All electrical-wiring work must be done by a licensed electrician, must follow the National Electric Code (NEC) and must be done according to codes set forth by the local building codes.

Electrical wiring can be tricky—especially for the novice. That's why it's usually best to hire a professional for anything other than a simple job. Otherwise, you could risk injury, damage or fire. If you do plan to complete a DIY project that has an electrical component, there are some basic things to know about wiring installation. Since the 1940s, any house built (or any older home that has been rewired) has had to follow an electrical code: the NEC—written with safety in mind.

NEC code identifies types of electrical wires and electrical cable types by color. When you remove a switch plate, you've probably noticed yellow, white, black, red or green wires. They are not there to be decorative; each serves a specific purpose, and some don't play nicely with others. When you're doing wiring installation, you need to identify the parts of the wiring cable, the non-metallic electrical cable: the outer sheathing (the jacket) and the inner wires.

The colored "wire" you see—the green, black, red, blue or white—is actually the sheathing that covers the inner copper wires. If you look closely, you'll see markings stamped on the sheathing to let you know the number and gauge of wires inside. The color of the sheathing lets you know what each wire does. The funny thing about electrics is that we never really worry about it until it malfunctions.

We don't think twice about turning on a computer, TV, or light. Instead, we expect it to work and ninety-nine times out of a hundred, it does. That said electrical malfunctions can and do happen, but when they do it's usually because of an underlying reason, typically your wiring. With this in mind, here are 5 answers to questions about electrical wiring you need to know. Electrical malfunctions cause more than 50,000 house fires each year, according to Electrical Safety Foundation International.

The majority can be prevented. To protect your own home, start by checking your fuse box or breaker panel for the date of your last inspection. Most municipalities require an inspection only when a system is modified during a renovation or an addition. However, the Consumer Product Safety Commission recommends having a pro look things over every 10 years. Beyond that, be aware of these potential sources and causes of electrical fires. Read on to explore more on electric wiring.

ALL ABOUT ELECTRICAL WIRING TYPES, SIZES & INSTALLATION

Much of what you need to know for electrical repairs and remodeling involves how to identify it, how to buy it, and how to install it with proper connections. If you're planning any electrical project, learning the basics of wiring materials and installation is the best place to start. Understanding basic wiring terminology and identifying the most common types of wire and cable will help when investigating wiring problems and when choosing the wiring for new installation and remodeling projects.

Here are all the basic elements you need to understand about electrical wiring.

Electrical wire sizes

The proper wire size is critical to any electrical wire installation. Wire sizing indicates the diameter of the metal conductor of the wire and is based on the American Wire Gauge (AWG) system. The gauge of a wire relates to the wire's current-carrying capacity, or how much amperage the wire can safely handle.

When choosing the right wire, you must consider the gauge of the wire, the wire capacity, and what the wire will be used for. Wires that are not properly matched to the amperage of the circuits they serve can create a notable risk of short circuit and fire.

Non-Metallic (NM) Sheathed Cable

Most interior wiring is done with non-metallic, or NM, cable—also known by the popular brand name Romex. NM cable is made of three or more wires wrapped inside a flexible plastic jacket, or sheathing. It is used for most interior circuits, such as those for outlets, switches, light fixtures, and appliances. Learn the basics of NM cable to choose the right type for your next electrical project.

Electrical Wire Color Coding

Color coding is used both on the outer sheathing of bundled electrical cables and on the individual conduction wires within cables or inside the conduit. Understanding this color coding can help you identify what the wiring is used for and helps maintain consistency within an electrical system. Cable coloring relates to the size of the wires inside the cable and the cable's amperage rating.

For example, white-sheathed NM cable is used for 15-amp circuits, while yellow NM cable is rated for 20-amp circuits. The coloring on individual conducting wires usually does not indicate a size or rating but rather the standard or preferred use of the wire.

For example, black and red wires typically are used for current-carrying or "hot" connections, and white wires usually are grounded "neutral" conductors. Green-insulated wires and bare copper wires are used for grounding wires.

Electrical Wiring Labeling

Electrical wires and cables have markings stamped or printed on their insulation or outer sheathing. These markings provide important information about the wiring and insulation, including the wire size and material, the type of insulation, the number of wires contained (inside a cable), and any special ratings or characteristics of the wire. While looking at the color of wire or cable will help you narrow down the options at the store, reading and understanding the labels on wiring is the best way to ensure you get the properly rated material for your project.

Direct-Burial Cable

Standard electrical cable is designed to be run indoors, where it stays dry and is protected by wall, ceiling, or floor structures. For outdoor projects or when running wiring underground, you must use direct-burial cable, which can be installed underground with or without conduit (depending on local building code rules). With direct-burial cable, the individual conducting wires are embedded in solid vinyl to fully protect them from moisture.

Electrical Wire Stripping

Stripping electrical wire involves removing the plastic insulation surrounding the wire's metal core. It's important to do this carefully so there is no damage to the metal. The procedure is simple but requires a special wire stripping tool and an understanding of how to use it. This is a critical skill—and tool—for DIYers to have for any wiring project.

Number of Wires Allowed in Conduit

When running individual electrical wires inside conduit, there is a limit to how many wires are allowed. The maximum allowable number is known as the "fill capacity," and this depends on several factors, including the size of the conduit, the gauge of the wires, and the conduit material. Metal (EMT), plastic (PVC), and flexible conduit all have different fill capacities, even when they're nominally the same size.

Wiring an Electrical Circuit Breaker Panel

The electrical panel, or service panel, is the power distribution point of a home electrical system. This is where all of the individual circuits of the house get their power and where they are protected by breakers or fuses. Wiring an electrical panel is a job for a licensed electrician, but DIYers should have a basic understanding of how a panel works and the critical role that breakers play in any system.

Electrical Disconnect Switches

An electrical disconnect switch provides a means to shut off the power to a home's electrical system from an outdoor location. It is typically mounted below the electric meter, either on the side of a home or on the utility company's power pole. This is a service disconnect switch. Not all homes have a dedicated disconnect. They are commonly used when the service panel (which also serves as the main disconnect) is located indoors and therefore is not accessible to emergency responders or utility workers.

Like electrical service panels, a disconnect must be installed by a licensed electrician.

Electrical Wiring Tips: What Is Hot, Neutral, and Ground

Before you perform any project or home improvement on your electrical system, you must have some understanding of how it works. Wiring is how electricity is distributed throughout your home, arguably making it the most crucial part of your electrical system. But how does wiring manage to transport electricity? The answer becomes clearer when we look at the three roles wiring must fulfill: hot, neutral, and ground.

These three components work in tandem to distribute power throughout your home, as well as help maintain electrical safety. It is recommended you understand each component's capabilities. For Milwaukee homeowners seeking electrical wiring tips, Roman Electric has assembled a guide on hot, neutral, and ground wire. Follow our guide below to better understand your electrical system!

Hot Wire

Hot wire is used as the initial power feed to a circuit. It carries the current from the power source to the outlet. Acting as the first instance of a circuit, they are always carrying electricity, meaning it is dangerous to touch a hot wire while there is a power source feeding it. Hot wire is identified by its black casing. This is the main color of hot wire for most homes. However, other hot wires can red, blue, or yellow, although these colors can indicate a different function besides powering an outlet. Regardless, all hot wire should be treated the same: do not touch hot wire unless there is no connected and operating power source.

Neutral Wire

Once hot wire has initialized the beginning of a circuit, there must be another wire to complete the circuit. This role is filled by neutral wire. Neutral wire carries the circuit back to the original power source. More specifically, neutral wire brings the circuit to a ground or busbar usually connected at the electrical panel. This gives currents circulation through your electrical system, which allows electricity to be fully utilized. Additionally, this prevents faulty or excess currents from residing in your outlet.

Neutral wires are identified by their white or gray casing. Although they may not always be circulating an electrical current, they should be handled with as much caution as hot wire.

Ground Wire

So, with hot and neutral already being used to make a circuit, what role is left? The answer is safety of course! Ground wire acts as defense against unstable electrical currents. Under normal circuit conditions, ground wire isn't carrying any current. But when an electrical accident such as a short circuit occurs, the ground wire takes the unstable current away from your electrical system and sends it toward the ground.

Ground wire is easily identified by its green casing. But not all homes may have it. Although it is a requirement by the NEC for newly-built homes, older homes don't always have a ground wire. To tell if your home has ground wire, check your outlets. If your outlets have three prongs, then your home has ground wire. If there are only two prongs, then ground wire may not be utilized.

If the latter is the case, we recommend consulting with Roman Electric to help determine if your home can be retrofitted with new ground wire.

8 Signs You May Have a Problem with Your Electrical Wiring

Only you can prevent house fires — or at least greatly lower the risk by keeping an eye out for these warning signs of trouble

1. Too many extension cords.

Aesthetics aside, there's a reason electric wires are buried within walls. "An undisturbed wiring system will more or less work forever," says William Burke, division manager of electrical engineering for the National Fire Protection Association. "But when it's disturbed or altered, there's potential for trouble." Running an extension cord creates additional points where cords can kink, short out or get pinched, leading to tripped breakers, damaged outlets or even a fire.

Use extension cords sparingly and for short periods of time — during the holidays, for example. If you consistently need more outlets, have an electrician install them.

2. Dimming or flickering lights.

Because light fixtures typically draw only a small amount of power, dimming or flickering is rarely caused by a problem with the fixture itself. More likely the issue is with energy hogs like major appliances or space heaters that are wired to the same circuit. "Appliances that heat or cool tend to draw a lot of power," says Burke. So dimming could be caused by a washing machine drawing current to heat water.

Consult an electrician about moving lights to different circuits or installing dedicated lines for major appliances.

3. Funny odors.

A new appliance may produce an off-odor the first few times it's powered up. But if you detect an odd smell coming from an outlet, turn off and unplug anything connected to it. Don't use it again until you've had a qualified electrician check it out. If your fuse box or breaker panel has a weird odor, call an electrician right away.

4. Sparking.

This is never a good sign. How you deal with it depends on where it's coming from. If a breaker panel, fuse box or outlet is sparking, get an electrician in ASAP. But a sparking appliance may mean that the fixture itself is damaged, in which case you should call an appliance repair person. He can test the appliance and usually the outlet that powers it as well. A service call from a repair person is likely to be cheaper than one from a licensed electrician. Plus, if the appliance is new, it may even be repaired under the warranty.

5. Hot outlets or switch plates.

Even when an appliance is meant to produce heat (like a toaster or space heater), the outlet that powers it should never become hot," says Burke. Electric current may make a switch plate slightly warm to the touch, but if the outlet is uncomfortably hot, turn off whatever is plugged in and try it in another outlet.

If the outlet grows hot even without anything plugged in, it may be wired incorrectly. Consult an electrician, who may advise you to flip the breaker or remove the fuse for that outlet until your system can be serviced.

6. Frequently blown fuses or tripped breakers.

Circuit breakers and fuses are designed to fail as a way to prevent overloading. If a vacuum cleaner or hair dryer routinely trips a breaker regardless of where you plug it in, the appliance is the likely culprit. But if using a single outlet causes you to blow the same fuse repeatedly, the circuit is probably overloaded. Call in a pro to discuss upgrading the circuit or adding a new line.

7. Buzzing.

What does electricity sound like? When things are working properly, nothing. Generally electricity flows smoothly and quietly between connections. But loose prongs, outlets or fraying wire can all cause the current to jump, producing a buzzing sound in the process. If you're sure a sound is originating at an outlet, stop using it and call an electrician.

8. The wrong outlets in the kitchen or bathroom.

Because water is an excellent conductor of electricity, kitchens and bathrooms both require special shock-resistant outlets called ground fault circuit interrupters (GFCIs). GFCIs typically have two small buttons at the center. If outlets in your kitchen or bathroom outlets look no different from those in your family room or bedroom, swap them out with GFCIs to add an extra layer of shock protection around water.

EXPOSED ELECTRICAL WIRING: CODE AND PRACTICES

One aspect of home wiring that electrical inspectors will pay close attention to is the improper use of non-metallic cable (NM) in exposed locations. Common exposed locations where this is found are on basement foundation walls or across the faces and ends of studs and joists in unfinished framed spaces. Learn if exposed wire is allowed, its dangers, and workarounds like THHN wire for exposed sheathed cables in your home.

Why Exposed Wire Should be Avoided

The National Electrical Code, the basis for all local building codes, has specific regulations for installing electrical wires so that they are protected

23

from damage to avoid fire, shocks, and trips or surges.

Fire: Exposed wire or any other wire that is insufficiently covered can cause fires if the wires short and result in a spark.

Shock: Exposed wire where the conductor is bare can shock a user, resulting in injury or death.

Trips, Surges: Exposed wires may not deliver sufficient power to devices, causing a higher power draw and tripped circuit breakers or short circuits.

NM Electrical Cable Proper Uses

Non-metallic or NM cable, also known by the trade name Romex, is the most common form of electrical wire used in residential electrical work. NM cable is a bundle of individual conducting wires wrapped in a plastic vinyl outer sheathing. Normally the cables carry 10-, 12-, or 14-gauge conducting wires for individual house circuits. The sheathing on NM cable does offer some protection against incidental physical damage.

Sheathing on Romex is made of tough polyvinyl chloride (PVC) thermoplastic. The sheathing on both 14 and 12 AWG wire is 19 mils thick. Still, no matter how strong the NM sheathing is, it is not meant for exposed applications.

Typical NM Wire Locations

Typical locations for NM cable include but are not limited to:

- ✓ Wall cavities that are covered with finished wall materials such as drywall or plaster, but only in cavities where the cable will not be accessible.
- ✓ Inside the air voids of masonry block or tile walls but only where the air voids are dry; the walls cannot be damp or wet.
- ✓ Between exposed joists or studs, provided the cables are recessed away from the face

of the framing members. This is normally done by boring holes in the centers of the framing members and running the cables through the holes.

NM Wire Improper Exposed Uses

The National Electrical Code forbids the use of NM cable in situations where it is exposed in a manner where physical damage is possible. One example of this is where a do-it-yourself electrician attaches NM cable across the front face of studs or ceiling joists or where it is attached across the face of concrete foundation walls. While it is allowable for NM cable to run through holes bored in the centers of exposed framing members, it cannot be attached across the front face of studs, since this creates the possibility of snagging or damage to the cables.

Similarly, NM attached to the face of concrete walls is susceptible to damage and thus is not allowed.

Wiring for Exposed Locations

One approved way to run wiring across exposed surfaces is to mount an approved rigid conduit across the framing members or wall, then run individual THHN conductor wires inside the conduit. Such wiring is well protected against physical damage. The citation from the National Electrical Code is as follows:

- ✓ Protection from Physical Damage: Cable shall be protected from physical damage where necessary by rigid metal conduit, intermediate metal conduit, electrical metallic tubing, Schedule 80 PVC conduit, Type RTRC marked with the suffix -XW, or other approved means.
- ✓ The most common type of conduit is known as electrical metallic tubing (EMT), but other types of conduit are also used, including flexible metal conduit (FMC), intermediate metal conduit (IMC), which is sturdier and offers more resistance to corrosion, plastic conduit (PVC), most often

used underground, and rigid metallic conduit (RMC), the heaviest gauge available.

✓ The electrical conduit is designed for use with specific types of individual conductor wires. The most common wires are THHN wires, which are individual copper conducting wires with a color-coded, heat-resistant plastic insulation around them.

How Many Wires Per Conduit?

The National Electrical Code has specific regulations for how many conductor wires can fit within a conduit of each diameter size:

✓ 1/2-inch Conduit: Up to 9 of the 12-gauge wires

✓ 1/2-inch Conduit: Up to 12 of the 14-gauge wires

✓ 3/4-inch Conduit: Up to 16 of the 12-gauge wires

✓ 3/4-inch Conduit: Up to 22 of the 14-gauge wires

Can NM Cable be Run Inside Conduit?

If an electrical inspector has flagged NM cable that has been run incorrectly, you might be tempted to install the conduit, then reuse the same NM cable by running it through the new conduit. This is a subject of some debate among electricians. Some pros argue that NM cable inside conduit may be susceptible to heat build-up and is therefore not allowed. Others take a more lenient view.

While the National Electrical Code does not expressly forbid inserting NM cable inside conduit, it is, in practice, very difficult to do so and very few professional electricians will do such an installation. It is the accepted practice to run only individual THHN conductors (or another approved form of wire) inside the conduit. THHN wires are relatively inexpensive and are much easier to run through conduit because they are thin and have less coating on them.

Tip

If THHN is being used, the conduit must run from termination point to termination point because THHN cannot be used outside the protection of conduit or another approved enclosure. If you run THHN cable inside a wall, which counts as an exposed area, there will need to be a transition point from the cable to the THHN, such as a junction box.

FAQ

Can you put Romex in conduit?

It is not good practice to put Romex in conduit. Romex is the brand name of a type of NM or non-metallic cable that is sheathed in tough, flexible plastic. Individually coated bundled wires are contained within the sheathing. It's generally best to run only separate THHN wires inside the conduit. THHN wires are inexpensive, easy to run through the conduit, and provide more space in the conduit since there is no cable sheathing or paper liner.

Can an exposed wire cause a fire?

An exposed wire can cause a fire. If the coating is nicked or if the live and ground wires touch, the resulting spark can cause a fire.

HOME ELECTRICAL BASICS

People depend on electricity constantly, and when the power goes out in a storm or there's a tripped breaker or another problem in an electrical circuit, understanding the basic components of an electrical system can help you get things running again. It's also important to know who is responsible for what portion of your electrical service.

The utility company handles the line portion of your service, which includes everything up to the attachment point on your house. From there, it's called the load side, and everything on the load side is your responsibility.

1. Electrical Service Connection and Meter

Your home's electricity starts with the power service and electric meter. The utility company's service cables (whether overhead or underground) extend to your house and connect to the utility's meter base. The electric meter plugs into this meter base. The meter measures the amount of electricity your home uses and is the basis for the charges on your electric bill. The meter runs only when electricity is used in the house.

2. Disconnect Switch

Some home electrical systems include a dedicated disconnect switch that is mounted on an outside wall of the home near the electric meter. In the event of a fire or flash flood, or if work needs to be done on the system, a disconnect switch allows you to shut off the power from outside the home so you don't have to enter the home to turn off the power. If an electrical system does not include a separate disconnect switch (and most do not), the main circuit breaker in the home's main service panel (breaker box) serves as the system disconnect.

3. Main Service Panel

After passing through the meter, your electrical service feeds into your home's main service panel, commonly known as the breaker box. Two large "hot" wires connect to big screw terminals, called lugs, inside the service panel, providing all the power to the panel. A third service wire, the neutral, connects to the neutral bus bar inside the panel. In simple terms, electricity is supplied to the house on the hot wires.

After it flows through the household system, it is fed back to the utility on the neutral wire, completing the electrical circuit.

4. Main Circuit Breaker

The service panel contains a large main breaker that is the switch controlling the power to the rest of the circuit breakers inside the panel. It is sized according to your home's service capacity. A standard panel today provides 200-amp (ampere) service. Older panels were sized for 150, 100, or fewer amps (amperes). A main breaker of 200 amps will allow a maximum of 200 amps to flow through it without tripping. In a tripped state, no current will flow to the panel.

In systems without an external disconnect switch, the main breaker serves as the household disconnect. Turning off the main breaker stops the flow of power to all of the branch circuit breakers in the panel, and therefore to all of the circuits in the house. However, power is always flowing into the panel and to the service lugs even when the main breaker is shut off unless the power is shut off at a separate disconnect switch.

Power is always present in the utility service lines and the electric meter unless it is shut off by the utility.

5. Branch Circuit Breakers

The breakers for the branch circuits fill the panel (usually below) the main breaker. Each of these breakers is a switch that controls the flow of electricity to a branch circuit in the house. Turning off a breaker shuts off the power to all of the devices and appliances on that circuit. If a circuit has a problem, such as an overload or a fault, the breaker automatically trips itself off.

The most common cause of a tripped breaker is a circuit overload. If you're running a high-demand appliance, such as a vacuum, toaster, or heater, and the power goes out, you've probably overloaded the circuit. Move the appliance to a different circuit and reset the breaker by switching it to the ON position. If the breaker trips again—without the appliance plugged in—you must call an electrician. There may be a dangerous fault situation in the circuit.

6. Devices

Devices are all the things in the house that are connected to electricity, including switches, receptacles (outlets), light fixtures, and appliances. Devices are connected to the individual branch circuits that start at the breakers in the main service panel. A single circuit may contain multiple switches, receptacles, fixtures, and other devices, or it may serve only a single appliance or receptacle.

The latter is called a dedicated circuit. These are used for critical-use appliances, such as refrigerators, furnaces, and water heaters. Other appliances, such as dishwashers and microwaves, usually are on dedicated circuits, too, so that they can be shut off at the service panel without interrupting service to other devices. This also reduces the incidence of overloaded circuits.

7. Switches

Switches are the devices that turn on and off lights and fans in your home. They come in many different styles and colors to suit your design needs. There are single-pole, three-way, four-way, and dimmer switches. When you flip a switch off, it "opens" the circuit, meaning the circuit is broken or not complete and the power is interrupted. When the switch is on, the circuit is "closed," and power flows beyond the switch to the light or another device it is controlling.

8. Outlets

Electrical outlets, technically called receptacles, provide power to plug-in devices and appliances. Televisions, lights, computers, freezers, vacuums, and toasters are all good examples of devices that can be plugged into an outlet. Standard outlets in a home are either 15-amp or 20-amp; 20-amp outlets can provide more electricity without tripping a breaker.

Special outlets for high-demand appliances, such as electric ranges and clothes dryers, may provide 30 to 50 or more amps of power. In potentially wet areas of a home, such as bathrooms, kitchens, and laundry rooms, some or all of the outlets must have GFCI (ground-fault circuit-interrupter) protection, provided by GFCI outlets or a GFCI breaker.

9. Wiring

Your home's wiring consists of a few different types of wiring, including non-metallic cable (commonly called Romex), Bx cable, and wiring concealed in conduit. NM cable is the most common type of circuit wiring. It is suitable for use in dry, protected areas (inside stud walls, on the sides of joists, etc.) that are not subject to mechanical damage or excessive heat. Bx cable, also known as armored cable, consists of wires running inside a flexible aluminum or steel sheath that is somewhat resistant to damage.

It is commonly used where wiring for appliances, such as dishwashers and garbage disposals, is exposed. Conduit is a rigid metal or plastic tubing that protects individual insulated wires. It is used in garages, sheds, and outdoor applications where the wiring must be protected from exposure. Wires running inside NM cable, Bx cable, or conduit are sized according to each circuit's amperage. Wire size is given in its gauge number.

The lower the gauge, the larger the wire, and the more current it can handle. For example, wiring for 20-amp circuits is 12-gauge, which is heavier than the 14-gauge wiring used for 15-amp circuits.

Romex Wire and NM Electrical Cable Buying Guide

The most common and efficient way of creating separated-wire bundles for residential electrical applications is by using NM (non-metallic) sheathed cable, such as the popular Romex brand. The copper wires that create individual circuits for residential electrical devices, such as GFCI outlets, lights, and wall outlets, generally run parallel in a tightly packed bundle, but they also must remain separate from one another, which is the function of Romex and other brands of NM sheathed electrical cable.

Romex is the brand name of a one type NM sheathed electrical cable made by Southwire Company, LLC of Carrollton, Georgia. Romex has become a somewhat generic term, often used to describe any and all brands of NM-sheathed electrical wire, but technically, it only refers to the cable made by Southwire Company.

The NM designation refers to the outer sheathing that bundles individual wires together like a cable. This is in contrast to metallic sheathed cable or conduit wiring, in which the bundle of individual conductors is protected by some form of a metal coil or metal conduit.

Cable Sheathing

NM electrical cable's outer sheathing is an extremely tough 30 mil-thick PVC jacket that serves to protect the bundle the individual wire conductors. The sheathing is necessary to withstand the stress inflicted when the cable is pulled through holes in the studs. It's now common practice for NM cable containing 14-gauge conductors to use a white outer jacket, for cable with 12-gauge conductors to use a yellow outer jacket, and for 10-gauge wire to use an orange or reddish jacket.

However, older NM cable may use a white outer jacket, regardless of the wire gauge of the individual conductors. To make connections with devices, cable sheathing is ripped laterally with a metal device called a cable ripper. At the end of the rip, the remaining attached sheathing is cut off with a utility knife, scissors, or the snipping portion of a wire stripper.

Wire Insulation

The individual wires (conductors) within the sheathing are insulated with color-coded PVC (polyvinyl chloride). The individual conductors normally have black, white, and red insulation. Also present within the NM cable is a copper grounding wire that is usually left uncoated and bare but sometimes is coated in green PVC. Often, a strip of paper is woven between the individual wires within the cable to serve as a separator. This paper can be snipped and discarded in the ripped portion of the cable.

Wires (Conductors)

Despite the NM label, the individual electrical conductors within the sheathing are indeed metal—normally a soft, uncoated copper that is usually at least 94 percent pure copper with some oxygen added during the fabrication process. These conductors are virtually identical to the THHN wires that are found inside rigid conduit. Some earlier forms of NM cable used aluminum or copper-jacketed aluminum, but these forms are no longer allowed by code—only pure copper wires are now used in residential wiring.

Wire Gauges

NM cable comes in many wire gauges, but most standard household circuits will use 12-gauge or 14-gauge wire, with either two or three conductors inside (plus the bare copper ground wire). Here are ratings per amps:

- ✓ **15 amps:** A cable labeled "14-2 with ground" will have two insulated conductors with 14-gauge wires plus a bare copper grounding wire. This cable is used for 15-amp circuits and often powers circuits from panels and individual devices.
- ✓ **20 amps**: A cable labeled "12-3 with ground" will have three 12-gauge insulated conductors (white, black, and red) plus the

bare copper grounding wire. A 12-gauge cable is rated for 20-amp circuits.

✓ **Over 30 amps**: For high-voltage circuits, such as 30- or 40-amp appliance circuits, even larger 10-gauge or 8-gauge NM cable may be required.

Tips

To connect to devices, wire insulation is stripped from the individual copper wire with a manual wire stripper. A series of holes in the wire stripper correlates with different wire diameters, or gauges. For example, choose the hole labeled "12" to strip the insulation from 12-gauge wire. Romex brand NM-sheathed is not the only brand of NM wire but it is the predominant brand in North American sales.

One feature of Romex is that it includes SIMpull, an embedded slippery coating on the sheathing that reduces friction when pulling the cable through studs and other difficult passages. Other brands have begun to incorporate a similar coating, as well. Other than this, there is no appreciable difference in the copper wire found in Romex when compared to other brands.

As required by electrical codes, the wire gauges will be the same and the metallic content the same, too. Professional electricians have individual preferences. One electrician might choose a cheaper brand, while another might prefer Romex. This poses no problem, as the various brands of NM cable can be mixed in the same electrical system or even in the same circuit.

Origin of Romex Brand Wire

The Romex name comes from Rome Cable Corp. of Rome, New York, which originally produced the cable (though the "x" in Romex remains a mystery). The company was an industry leader until it filed for bankruptcy in 2003 and its factory was largely demolished in 2010. Rome Cable Corp. was also a major source of aluminum wire produced by its parent company Alcoa.

Aluminum wire is inferior to copper wire and its presence is considered to be dangerous in your home. In 1964, Alcoa was court-ordered to divest itself of Rome Cable Corp.

NM Wiring Pros and Cons

NM wiring is very common in residential wiring, but it is also possible to wire a home using metallic sheathed cable or conduit. NM wiring has many advantages that make it the most popular type of wiring, especially for homeowners. With all factors considered, do-it-yourself electricians will find their projects easier and cheaper to complete when using NM wiring. NM wiring presents a huge amount of advantages to the do-it-yourselfers, as opposed to other materials.

Pros

- ✓ NM wire can be installed in plastic boxes and does not require the extra step of grounding the box itself.
- ✓ NM wire is lighter than metallic sheathed wiring, so it is easier to handle.
- ✓ NM wire is easier to unspool and straighten out because the PVC sheathing is pliable.
- ✓ It is easier to pull through holes in studs because of the smooth sheathing. In the case of Romex, a coating is added that makes the sheathing more slippery.
- ✓ NM cable is easier to cut with just a set of side-cutting pliers. Smaller gauges can even be snipped with the wire stripper.
- ✓ NM wire is cheaper than metal-sheathed wiring.
- ✓ NM cable is easier to rip since the sheathing is plastic, not metal. Though a ripping tool makes your job easier, you can also cut the

sheathing with a utility knife and rip it back by hand.

✓ NM cable is easier to attach to framing members, requiring only lightweight plastic cable staples.

Cons

✓ There are situations in which NM cable cannot be used, such as outdoors (except for UF-type cable, which is rated for direct burial) or when wiring is exposed along the face of foundation walls. In these instances, the electrical code calls for conduit installations.

✓ NM cable also needs to have some sort of protection in certain applications, or when not inside a wall.

✓ NM cable also cannot be used above drop ceilings in light commercial applications.

ELECTRICAL WIRING COLOR

CODING SYSTEM

Electrical wire color codes are part of a standard system that tells the user which wires carry a current and which wires are for ground or neutral purposes. For example, black and red wires (or white wires taped with either of these colors) are hot wires that carry current. Bare copper or green wires are used as ground wires. White or gray indicates neutral wires. Understanding the color coding for electrical wiring will help you know the purpose of each wire to keep you safe and your house's electrical system in top working order.

What Are Wire Color Code Standards?

The United States follows the National Electrical Code® (NEC), a system for electrical standards that includes partial guidance on electrical wire colors. The NEC says that white or gray must be used to identify neutral conductors and that bare copper or green should be used to identify ground wires. Knowing these colors helps you safely identify the type of electrical wire, its purpose, and how it will power an appliance or circuit.

Color Markings: Cable Sheathing and Wires

Non-metallic (or NM) 120-volt and 240-volt electrical cables come in two main parts: the outer plastic sheathing (or jacket) and the inner, color-coded wires.

Cable Sheathing

The sheathing is a tough outer coat that binds the inner wires together. The color of the sheathing indicates the gauges (or thicknesses) of the wires inside.

✓ White: White sheathing means that the inner wires are 14-gauge wires intended for 15-amp service, used often for light circuits and some receptacle circuits.

- ✓ Yellow: Yellow sheathing indicates that the wires are 12-gauge wires intended for 20-amp service, typically used for GFCI outlet circuits.
- ✓ Orange: Orange sheathing means that the wires are 10-gauge wires intended for 30 amp service for larger devices like water heaters, air conditioners, or dryers.
- ✓ Black: This is typically used for even larger devices that require 40 amps to 60 amps, such as ranges, air handlers (with electric heating elements), or to sub-feed a sub-panel.

Printed numbers and words on the sheathing tell you the number and the gauges of the wires within the sheathing.

Wire Color Codes

Within the sheathing is a different set of wire color codes that has another meaning: the wire's purpose and, incidentally, its potential danger.

Wire color codes are black, red, white, bare copper, green, white or gray, and blue or yellow. White, gray, bare copper, and green are the only wire colors that the NEC mandates must indicate a specific purpose.

White or gray must be used for neutral conductors. Bare copper or green wires must be used as ground wires. Beyond that are general, industry-accepted rules about wire color codes that indicate their purpose.

Electrical Wiring Color Coding System

Black Wires: Hot

Black insulation is always used to designate hot wires. This is commonly found in most standard household circuits. The term "hot" is used for source wires that carry power from the electric service panel to a destination, such as a light or an outlet. Even though you are permitted to use a white wire as a hot wire by marking it with electrical tape, the opposite is not recommended or allowed. In other words, do not use a black wire as a neutral or ground wire, or for any purpose other than for carrying live electrical loads.

Red Wires: Hot

Red insulation is used to designate hot wires. Red wires are sometimes used as the second hot wire in 240-volt installations. Another useful application for red wires is to interconnect hardwired smoke detectors so that if one alarm is triggered all of the others go off simultaneously. The other common use for the red wire is switching. In a circuit where multiple switches turn a light on and off from different locations, the red wire provides for this option.

White Wires With Black or Red Tape: Hot

White wire insulation augmented with a red or black color marking usually indicates that it is being used as a hot wire rather than as a neutral wire. Typically, this is indicated with a band of black or red electrical tape wrapped around the wire's insulation. Sometimes other colors are used, as well. For instance, a white wire in a two-wire cable may be used for the second hot wire on a 240-volt appliance or outlet circuit.

This white wire should be looped several times around with black electrical tape to show that it is being used for something other than a neutral.

Bare Copper Wires: Ground

Bare copper is the most common type of wire color code to indicate a ground wire. Bare copper is the only wire color code that is not found on plastic wire insulation; it is simply the wire itself, devoid of insulation. All electrical devices must be grounded. In the event of a fault, grounding provides a safe route for electricity to travel to ground, instead using your body as the route.

Bare copper wires connect to electrical devices, such as switches, outlets, and fixtures, as well as metal appliance frames or housings. Metal electrical boxes also need ground connection because they are made of a conductive material. Plastic boxes are non-conductive and do not need to be grounded.

Green Wires: Ground

Green plastic insulation is sometimes used to indicate ground wires. Ground screws on electrical devices are often painted green, too. Never use a green wire for any purpose other than for grounding.

White or Gray Wires: Neutral

White or gray wire insulation indicates a neutral wire. When examining a white or gray wire, make certain that it has not been wrapped in electrical tape. This would indicate a hot wire. Older wires sometimes may lose their electrical tape wrapping.

So, if the box has a loose loop of tape inside of it, there is the possibility that it may have come off of the neutral wire. The term neutral can be dangerously deceiving as it appears to imply a non-electrified wire.

It is important to note that neutral wires may also be carrying power and can shock you. While wires designated as hot (black or red insulated wires) carry power from the service panel (breaker box) to the device, neutral wires carry power back to the service panel. Thus, both hot and neutral wires have the potential to shock and injure you.

Blue and Yellow Wires

Blue and yellow wire insulation is sometimes used to indicate hot wires inside an electrical conduit. Rarely are blue and yellow wires found within NM cable sheathing. Blue wires are commonly used for travelers in three-way and four-way switch applications.

Benefits of Standard Wire Color Codes

Understanding and using standard wire color coding in electrical projects is important for safety, code requirements, and for more efficient organization of future electrical projects. Using the wrong color codes will make you less safe because you are at a greater risk of shock. Your home is less safe, too, because improperly connected wires may cause a fire.

Being aware of electrical wire colors is valuable, too, since the electrical code requires that certain wires (neutral and ground) follow a standard color coding pattern. Color-coded electrical wires help you with future projects and make them easier to accomplish since you don't have to figure out the purpose of each wire. Each wire's purpose is labeled for you.

CONDUIT FOR ELECTRICAL WIRING

When we talk about conduits, we are talking about pipes that are used to conduit electrical wiring through buildings. These conduits can be installed indoors or outdoors and there are a number of reasons why you should be using conduits for your electrical wiring. In this article, we will explain the purpose of electric conduits, and when are the right times to use them.

Electrical Conduit

An electrical conduit is simply a pipe that is designed to conduct electricity. These pipes are used for a number of different purposes including building interiors and electrical wiring. Conduit pipes are used in order to protect your home or business from an electric fire, as well as for aesthetic reasons (such as the look of the buildings).

Also, conduits can be used to route electrical wiring, such as in commercial and residential buildings. Conduits are often made from PVC plastic, galvanized steel, aluminum or copper. All of these metals are good conductors of electricity and will not allow the electric current to flow through the pipe but can still carry the electricity safely through the building. Some people even use stainless steel as a conduit because it is more durable than galvanized steel.

Electrical conduit pipes are made in a number of different sizes and they can be used indoors or outdoors. Conduits are usually used to protect your home from a fire caused by electrical wiring, but they can also be used for aesthetic reasons. Conduits can be made from plastics, galvanized steel, aluminum, copper, or stainless steel.

Purpose of Electrical Conduit

The purpose of an electrical conduit is to be able to adequately protect your home or business from electrocution, as well as for the aesthetic purposes of your building. In addition, electrical conduits are used for this purpose because they can allow different wires to safely run through the same pipe; this is especially important when it comes to large heavy equipment such as electric motors, generators and other exposed wiring.

Additionally, these pipes can be used as a way to expand electrical wiring inside your home or business, and they can be used when you are rewiring a building. The right time to use an electrical conduit is when you are manually running wire for electricity, or when re-wiring a building. Before using a conduit, be sure to check your local building codes and regulations; there are sometimes restrictions on how to install one.

Where are Cables and Conduits Used?

Cable conduits and electrical conduits are used in a number of different ways, but the most common way is to use them inside of a house. When installing these conduits, make sure to use conduit support; this is simply a piece that is installed into the pipe itself. This is not only important for the stability of the conduit, but it is also especially important because these conduits can become very heavy when they are covered in wires and cables.

Also, you can use these conduits for the main electrical wiring in your home (in addition to using electrical junction boxes). However, you need to make sure that all of your conduit pipes are properly grounded; this will help prevent an electric fire from occurring. Lastly, they are used in commercial buildings. In addition, an electrical conduit can be used on the outside of a building as well.

The outside use of these conduits is especially useful in order to protect a building from falling debris and other damage that might occur on the outside of a building.

Can Wire be Buried without Conduit?

Although you can bury wires without the use of conduits, you should never do it. If you are looking to bury wires, make sure that you use an expert to ensure that this is done correctly; burying electrical conduits or cables is a very difficult process. The reason behind this is because the ground itself has an electrical resistance and if the soil becomes wet and moist enough – then it could create an open circuit.

Additionally, electricians cannot bury wires without the use of a lightning arrestor, as these are designed to slow down a lightning bolt. The reason behind this is because they work to break the flow of electricity created by a lightning bolt; this prevents damage to your electrical system.

Choosing The Right Electrical Conduits for Your Home or Office

When you are looking to buy a pair of electrical conduits, you should look for several different things in order to make sure that they are the correct ones for your purpose. The first thing that needs to be considered is the function of the trunking, such as whether it is convenient to install and disassemble, whether the fire resistance or insulation performance is good, whether it is easy to bend, whether it is moisture-proof and acid-base resistant, etc.

It is also important that you understand what type of pipe these conduits are made from. You should also try to find out about the material that the electrical conduit is made from; this will give you an idea of how long it will last before it needs to be replaced. Also, you should make sure that you do not buy conduits that are wrapped with asbestos, as this material contains small fibers that can be released into the air if they are exposed to high amounts of heat.

Summary

Electrical conduits or Cables are used for a variety of different purposes, which include being used to safely run wires through the interior of your home, as well as wiring up large electrical equipment such as motors, generators, and air conditioners. You can use these pipes outdoors or indoors and they can be made from several different metals.

When burying wiring with a LESSO conduit, make sure not to do it if you are not willing to have the work professionally done. Also, know the different materials that are used in the making of these pipes; this will help ensure that you select a high-quality pipe for your purpose. The most important aspect when keeping wires safe and grounded is to make sure that they are correctly connected and stay connected throughout the duration of your home or office.

To ensure this, there are numerous types of LESSO electrical conduit available, depending on your project's needs.

Different Types of Electrical Wire and How to Choose One

Electrical wire is typically made of copper or aluminum, and these conductive materials are insulated as wires that bring electricity to various parts of your home. When you're installing new wiring, choosing the right wire or cable is half the battle. On the other hand, when examining the old wiring in your home, identifying the wire type can tell you a lot about the circuit the wiring belongs to (for example, if you open a junction box and need to determine which wires go where).

Wiring for modern homes is quite standard, and most homes built after the mid-1960s have similar types of wiring. Any new electrical installation requires new wiring that conforms to local building codes. Below, learn the different types of home electrical wires to choose the right option for completing electrical projects accurately and safely.

Wiring Terminology

It helps to understand a few basic terms used to describe wiring. An electrical wire is a type of -conductor, which is a material that conducts electricity. In the case of household wiring, the conductor itself is usually copper or aluminum (or copper-sheathed aluminum) and is either a solid metal conductor or stranded wire. Most wires in a home are insulated, meaning they are wrapped in a nonconductive plastic coating.

One notable exception is ground wires, which are typically solid copper and are either insulated with green sheathing or uninsulated (bare).

Note: Many larger wires in your home are carrying 120- to 240-volt circuit voltage, often referred to as line voltage, and they can be very dangerous to touch. There are also several wires in your home that carry much lesser amounts of "low-voltage" current. These are less dangerous, and with some, the voltage carried is so low that there is virtually no chance of shock. However, until you know exactly what kind of wires you are dealing with, it's best to treat them all as dangerous.

1. NM Cable

Best For: Interior Use In Dry Locations

Often called "Romex" after one popular brand name, nonmetallic (NM) cable is a type of circuit wiring designed for interior use in dry locations. NM is the most common type of wiring in modern homes. It consists of two or more individual wires wrapped inside a protective plastic sheathing. NM cable usually contains one or more "hot" (current-carrying) wires, a neutral wire, and a ground wire.

These conductors are insulated in white (usually neutral) and black (usually hot) for installation. Most NM cables have a flattened tubular shape and run invisibly through the walls, ceiling, and floor cavities of your home.

Tip

As an alternative to NM cable, individual wires can be installed inside of a rigid or flexible metal or plastic tubing called conduit. Conduit is typically used where the wiring will be exposed and not hidden inside walls, floors, or ceilings. Almost all of the wiring in outlets and light fixtures in a modern home is NM cable. This type of wire is used for hidden applications in the walls, as it is cheaper than using a conduit. The most common sizes and their amperage (amp) ratings are:

- ✓ 14-gauge (15-amp circuits)
- ✓ 12-gauge (20-amp circuits)
- ✓ 10-gauge (30-amp circuits)
- ✓ 8-gauge (40-amp circuits)
- ✓ 6-gauge (55-amp circuits)

NM cable is now sold with a color-coded outer jacket to indicate its wire gauge:

- ✓ White sheathing indicates NM cable with 14-gauge conductors.
- ✓ Yellow sheathing indicates NM cable with 12-gauge conductors.
- ✓ Orange sheathing indicates NM cable with 10-gauge conductors.
- ✓ Black-sheathed cable is used for both 6- and 8-gauge wire.
- ✓ Gray sheathing is not used for NM cable but is reserved for underground (UF) cable or service entrance cable (SE or SER).
- ✓ NM cable is dangerous to handle while the circuit conductors are carrying voltage.

2. UF Cable

Best For: Underground Wire For Outdoor Fixtures

Underground Feeder (UF) is a type of nonmetallic cable designed for wet locations and direct burial in the ground. It is commonly used for supplying outdoor fixtures, such as lampposts. Like standard NM cable, UF contains insulated hot and neutral wires, plus a bare copper ground wire. But while sheathing on NM cable is a separate plastic wrap, UF cable sheathing is solid plastic that surrounds each wire.

This type of electrical wire is also a bit more expensive than NM wire because of its durable insulation. UF cable is normally sold with gray outer sheathing. UF cable is also used for major circuit wiring, and it carries a dangerous amount of voltage as long as the circuits are turned on.

3. THHN/THWN Wire

Best For: Insulated Wire Inside Conduits

THHN and THWN are codes for the two most common types of insulated wire used inside conduit. Unlike NM cable, in which two or more individually insulated conductors (copper or aluminum) are bundled inside a plastic sheathing, THHN and THWN wires are single conductors, each with its color-coded insulation. Instead of being protected by NM cable sheathing, these wires are protected by tubular metal or plastic conduit.

Conduit is often used in unfinished areas, such as basements and garages, and for short exposed runs inside the home, such as wiring connections for garbage disposers and hot water heaters. These wires typically have similar prices to NM wire (plus the cost of the conduit). The letters indicate specific properties of the wire insulation:

- ✓ T: Thermoplastic
- ✓ H: Heat-resistant; HH means highly heat-resistant
- ✓ W: Rated for wet locations
- ✓ N: Nylon-coated, for added protection

THHN and THWN wires have colored sheathings that are generally used to identify their function in a circuit:

- ✓ Hot wires: Black, red, orange
- ✓ Neutral wires: White, brown
- ✓ Ground wires: Green, yellow-green

THHN and THWN wires are circuit wires that should never be handled when the circuits are turned on.

4. Low-Voltage Wire

Best For: Circuits Requiring 50 Volts Or Less

Low-voltage wiring is used for circuits typically requiring 50 volts or less. Several common types are landscape lighting wire, sprinkler system connections, bell wire (for doorbells), speaker system wires, and thermostat wires. Wire sizes range from about 22 gauge to 12 gauge, and these wires can be made of copper or aluminum. Low-voltage wires typically are insulated and may be contained in cable sheathing or combined in twisted pairs, similar to lamp cord wire.

It must be used only for low-voltage applications. These are typically very small wires that are much different from standard circuit wiring, and their costs tend to be lower than other household wires. Serious shocks rarely occur with low-voltage wires, but it is still always best to turn off devices before working with them.

5. Phone and Data Wire

Best For: Landline Telephones And Internet Hookups

Telephone and data wiring are low-voltage wires used for "landline" telephones and internet hookups, typically made from copper. Telephone cables may contain four or eight wires. Category 5 (Cat 5) cable, the most common type of household data wiring, contains eight wires wrapped together in four pairs. It can be used for both phone and data transmission and offers greater capacity and quality than standard phone wire.

Like low-voltage wire, it is often cheaper than other types of household wiring like NM or UF cables.

Although data wiring does carry a small amount of voltage, anything under 30 volts is generally regarded as safe (a household circuit carries about 120-volts of power).1 However, there is always a danger of data wiring coming into contact with household wiring, so you should treat it with caution and avoid touching bare wires.

6. Coaxial Cable

Best for: Data wiring

Coaxial cable is beginning to grow less common, thanks to the use of other forms of data wiring, such as HDMI, for television data transmission. Coaxial cable is a round, jacketed cable that features an inner conductor (usually copper) surrounded by a tubular insulating layer, surrounded by a tubular conducting shield made of braided wire.

It can be identified by the threaded connectors that are used to make unions and device hookups.

Coaxial cable was once the standard for connecting televisions to antenna or cable service delivery and is still often used to connect satellite dishes or to bring subscription television service to an in-home distribution point. It typically has black or white insulation and is perfectly round in shape, making it easy to distinguish from NM electrical circuit cables.

Coaxial cable can be found for affordable prices at most hardware and electronics stores. The minuscule amount of voltage carried by coaxial cable signals makes it very unlikely to cause a shock of any type—provided the cables are not in contact with another source of current.

Choosing a Type of Electrical Wire

Whether you're replacing old wiring in your home or adding new electrical wires, it's important to choose the right type. Always select an electrical wire that is specified for the purpose you intend to use it for. For example, in wet locations outdoors,

UF wire should always be chosen to ensure that your home's electrical system is protected from the elements.

The amperage and volts of each wire should also be considered, and wires should be matched to the correct needs of every electrical project. If you're unsure which type of electrical wire you need, it's helpful to consult a professional electrician before installing any sort of electrical lines in your home.

20 TOP TOOLS YOU MAY NEED FOR ELECTRICAL PROJECTS

Electrical tools are required for repairs or improvement projects around the house. For most residential electrical projects, you'll use primarily basic hand tools you already own, such as a hammer, tape measure, laser level, flathead, and Phillips screwdrivers. Some specialty electrical tools like voltage testers, wire strippers, and linesman pliers come in handy from time to time, and these are readily available at most home centers, hardware stores, electrical supply stores, and online retailers.

Various Electrical Tools

Things like voltmeters, fish tape, and flashlights can be helpful when doing an at-home project. As with any tool purchase, you'll get longer life and better performance from higher-quality tools. Better electrical hand tools, such as wire cutters and linesman pliers, have insulated handles to help guard against shock.

1. Non-Contact Voltage Tester

Perhaps the most crucial specialty electrical tool you can own is a voltage tester. A voltage tester is used for a quick safety check to ensure no current is flowing to an electrical wire or device before you start working on it. Powered by batteries, non-contact voltage testers are the simplest and safest testers because they can detect electricity near an outlet slot or wire. This is a tool every DIYer needs in the toolbox. It will be used for virtually every home electrical repair project.

2. Wire Strippers

Another essential electrical specialty tool for homeowners is a good pair of wire strippers. Wire strippers are used to cut and strip insulation from electrical wires. A wire stripper tool has a row of gauged holes for stripping wires of different sizes, and it usually includes cutting jaws for trimming the wire ends. Some types are combination tools that crimp wires and strip the vinyl jacket off NM cable (non-metallic sheathed cable).

This is perhaps the most essential specialty electrical tool you can own, along with a voltage tester. It makes sense to invest in a good set of wire strippers, as it will serve many functions.

3. Tape Measure

A standard tape measure is used for all field measurements, such as setting heights for switches and outlets, centering lighting fixture boxes, and marking surfaces for cutouts.

4. Hammer

A hammer is used to secure electrical boxes equipped with nail-on brackets to wall studs and other framing members in a home. You'll also need one to drive wire staples when anchoring new electrical cables to framing members.

5. Voltmeter or Multimeter

A voltmeter reads voltage levels and verifies that circuits are "live" or off. Unlike a circuit tester, this tool reads how much voltage is being carried. More sophisticated forms of the device are known as multimeters, and they can read voltage levels, amperage, resistance, and DC voltage and amperage. However, they require practice to learn how to use them properly.

This specialty tool is used mainly by advanced DIYers and professional electricians. Casual DIYers may not need to own this tool, but those who do a lot of electrical work on appliances and electronics may find it essential.

6. Torpedo Level

A small level, such as a torpedo level, fits easily in a tool pouch and ensures your work is level and plumb. A great installation starts with level boxes and straight switch and outlet receptacles. A torpedo level should be part of every homeowner's standard toolkit; it will have plenty of uses beyond electrical work.

7. Flashlight

Electrical repair and improvement work involves a lot of dark places, from attics and basements to wall and ceiling cavities, to the insides of electrical boxes. A tactical flashlight is needed as much for safety as for convenience. A few hand flashlights and a headlamp are good additions to a DIY electrician's toolbox.

8. Utility Knife

A utility knife, or box cutter, is handy for cutting sheathing from non-metallic (Romex) cable, cutting off electrical tape, and opening cardboard boxes.

9. Phillips Screwdrivers

Electricians keep screwdrivers with them at all times for removing and installing cover plates, outlets, switches, and many other devices. It's best to have a few different lengths of Phillips screwdrivers and #1, #2, and #3 tip sizes. Screwdrivers with insulating rubber jackets covering the handles are designed for better safety when doing electrical work.

10. Straight-Blade Screwdrivers

As with Phillips screwdrivers, you will likely need more than one size of straight-blade screwdriver. If you have to choose just one, pick a medium blade; it will suit most projects. Straight-blade screwdrivers are also available with insulated handles for better safety when doing electrical work.

11. Allen Wrench Set (Hex Set)

Allen wrenches are used to tighten hex-head screws, which are sometimes found on ceiling fans, light fixtures, and appliances. Owning a metric and a standard set of Allen wrenches is a good idea.

12. Tongue-and-Groove Pliers

Tongue-and-groove pliers are known by many names, including channel-lock, groove joint, and straight-jaw pliers. This tool is often used for plumbing work, but a pair of tongue-and-groove pliers also has many uses for electrical projects. It will frequently remove knockouts from metal electrical boxes, tighten cable clamps, and adjust expansion-type ceiling fan boxes.

13. Needle-Nose Pliers

Another essential specialty electrical tool is a pair of needle-nose pliers (also called long-nose pliers). It will be used for bending and twisting wires when making screw-terminal connections. The long, narrow tip makes this an excellent tool for detailed work. Most needle-nose pliers also include cutting jaws for trimming wires.

14. Linesman Pliers

A pair of linesman pliers is an electrician's do-it-all tool. It has a squared-off end that is great for twisting wires together, a center cutting blade for trimming wire, and a grip area between the handles for pulling wire. Casual DIYers may be able to get by without this tool, but anyone who does regular electrical work will want to own a pair of linesman pliers.

15. Diagonal Cutting Pliers

Diagonal cutting pliers, sometimes called side snips or dikes, are used to cut wires. They are specially designed with a cutting edge that goes down to the tip of the jaws, allowing you to get into tight areas to trim wires. Some types are sold in a pair along with a voltage detector to sense live wires. You can also find combination tools, including wire-stripping slots built into the handles. This is a second-tier specialty tool: Casual DIYers may not need it, but those who do regular electrical work will find it very useful.

16. Fish Tape

Fish tape pulls stranded or solid wire conductors through metal or PVC conduit. Cable lube can assist you in removing the wires through the conduit. Fish tape can also be helpful when pulling NM cable through wall cavities. This tool is used when making wiring improvements, such as adding or extending circuits. Casual DIYers who make electrical repairs or replacements rarely need fish tape, but it is a good tool for more advanced DIYers to own.

17. Wire Crimpers

Wire crimpers are used to crimp lugs or connection terminals onto wires. This tool is not often used for routine circuit repairs but has many uses when working with appliances or electronics. Many types can also be used to strip wire insulation. This specialty tool is not needed by every DIYer since some of the key functions can be performed by other tools you already have. But if you routinely work on appliances, it can be a helpful tool.

18. Cable Tracers

When there's a jumble of wires, and you're unsure if the connected wire you're looking at is the one you need, a cable finder or tracer will quickly find cable and wire paths. A cable tracer uses a transmitter and a receiver, or toner and probe, to send a signal down the cable, which you can pinpoint using the receiver. This tool can be used on telecommunications, electrical, coaxial, or network lines.

It's inexpensive, easy to use, and available online and in most home improvement stores. Note: This tool differs from a cable locator, which is a device that detects wires through walls or underground.

19. Electric Screwdriver

An electric screwdriver is a portable device that can screw and unscrew using a battery or corded power. These tools are handy for more extensive projects versus manual screwdrivers, especially when you have many screws to be installed or removed. This tool is smaller but similar to a power drill. It does not do everything a drill can; it's only used for screws.

Like a drill, the screwdriver and the bit holder can be magnetic or screwed in, accommodating different sizes and types of screwdriver heads. A corded drill is usually more powerful, and you don't have to worry about losing time charging the battery. However, a battery-operated model allows you to be out of range from a plug or when you need more manual dexterity, such as furniture assembly.

20. Coaxial Cable Compression Tool

For less than $20, a coaxial cable compression tool is helpful when doing cable work around the house or running coax to a TV antenna. This easy-to-use coax crimper tool helps you replace F connectors or repair a coax line so that TV and internet connections are strong without any leakage.

FAQ

How do I shut off the electric in my house?

If you want to turn off the electric to the entire house, go to your home's service panel box and flip the switch for the main breaker to off.

Why did the circuit breaker trip?

Circuit breakers can trip for a few reasons. The most common reason a circuit breaker trips is because of an overload. It can also trip due to a short circuit, ground circuit, or Arc fault.

Where do GFCI outlets need to be installed in a house?

GFCI outlets should be installed in bathrooms, kitchens, laundry rooms of all homes and the National Electric Code (NEC) requires them in garages and basements or where receptacles are within six feet of water in new construction.

What Is Non-Metallic (NM) Electrical Cable?

No matter what brand of NM cable you purchase, there are typically three parts to the cable: outer cable sheathing, wire insulation, and individual wires (conductors). Here's a more in-depth look.

Printed in Great Britain
by Amazon

40958138R00056